Old Stockton-on-Tees

including
Norton and Thornaby

Paul Chrystal

Text © Paul Chrystal, 2020.
First published in the United Kingdom, 2020,
by Stenlake Publishing Ltd.,
54-58 Mill Square,
Catrine, Ayrshire,
KA5 6RD

Telephone: 01290 551122
www.stenlake.co.uk

ISBN 9781840338652

Printed by Blissetts,
Roslin Road,
Acton,
W3 8DH

The publishers regret that they cannot supply copies of any pictures featured in this book.

For Paul and Angela

Stockton Castle, previously just Stockton Hall. The Castle Theatre opened in 1908 on the site of the old castle and was demolished in 1969. The site was later occupied by the Swallow Hotel which closed in 2009, its former presence indicated by Tower Street and the Castle Gate Shopping Centre. Some of the stonework from the old castle may have been incorporated into Stockton's Green Dragon Yard, Finkle Street and Silver Street just off the High Street.

Introduction

Stockton has its origins with the Anglo Saxons and was described in the *Boldon Book* of 1183 as having 'eighteen farms, three families with a cottage but little land, a smith and a ferry across the River Tees'. The *Boldon Book* (also the *Boldon Buke*) published the results of a survey of the bishopric of Durham completed on the orders of Hugh du Puiset, Bishop of Durham, designed to assist the administration of the vast diocesan estates. The *Boldon* was not unlike the *Domesday Book* of the previous century, covering the bishop's lands in what was to become County Durham and other parts of the north east of England. After the Norman Conquest these lands were liable to tax by the Prince-Bishop of Durham and not taxed directly by the King of England.

Later, Bishop Pudsey of Durham (Hugh de Puiset c.1125–95), made his residence in Bishop's Hall, a glorified, fortified manor house. The only known relic of this is a wrought stone, about three feet in length, on which are the figures of two couchant lions. This stone was formerly part of the wall of a cow-byer in Hartburn, but afterwards placed in the grounds of "the late Colonel Sleigh at Elton". Archaeological excavations in the 1960s before the construction of the Swallow Hotel revealed high status Norman stonework dating from 1150-1170AD. These stones would have been part of the hall. King John stayed here in 1200AD, 1210AD and 1212AD. The Bishop's Hall was rebuilt in 1316AD and a moat was dug around it. From then on it was called a castle.

During the Civil War Stockton Castle was a Royalist stronghold and in 1640 when a treaty was signed making the Tees a boundary between the forces of Scotland and the English King, the castle stayed in Royalist hands. Scottish forces under the Earl of Callendar finally captured it in 1644 and the castle was garrisoned by them until 1646. In 1647 the House of Commons gave the order that the castle be 'made untenable and the garrison disgarrisoned'. Only the castle barn, a 'castellated cowhouse', remained until its demolition in 1865.

In the 1660s Stockton was a town of houses of thatch and timber probably generally run down and dilapidated. However, from about 1680 to 1710 there was a renaissance which saw major rebuilding of the houses using brick and tiles some of which may have been salvaged from the castle. Stockton's improving status was reflected in the relocation of the Customs Office from Hartlepool to Red Lion Yard, Stockton in 1680. In 1771 the Bishop's Ferry was replaced by a five arch stone bridge – the lowest bridging point of the Tees until the Middlesbrough Transporter Bridge opened in 1911. The bridge opened up markets in Cleveland and reinforced Stockton as a market town, reducing journeys by six miles as it obviated the need for travellers to use the Yarm Bridge. The 18th century saw Stockton boom as a commercial centre as evidenced by 28-29 Silver Street which are typical small houses of that period, although now heavily re-built with modern shops, including Drake – the bookshop. Silver Street and Silver Court were named after the silversmiths who used to work from here. Addresses like 16 Church Road are high status town houses built for wealthy merchants and professionals. The famous Town House (now known as the Town Hall) was built in 1735; renovations in the 1990s revealed that some parts of the building are even older, probably dating from a lock-up on the same site as a Town House has existed on that site perhaps as far back as 1100. The first reference to it is in *Hatfield's Survey* from 1382, when a plot of land available for the Manor (the site of the Town House) existed on payment of 4 pennies per year to the Bishops of Durham. The Town House, described as a 'mean building', was in effect the mayor's house which received rents, tolls, fines and admittances to the market.

In the 1600s this building housed guests of the borough and was still described as 'mean'. After the boom of the Restoration this thatched cottage was abandoned and a purpose-built tolbooth was built to the south of it. Proclamations were read from steps on the ground floor. The first floor was built on open arches and contained a long room (now used as a committee room) in which tolls were paid and meetings of burgesses were held. The tolbooth housed a small lock-up used to detain drunkards, scolds and blaggards along with those awaiting escort to Durham charged with more serious offences. To the west of the tolbooth were the stocks and the whipping post. It was not until the early 1800s that anyone expressed concern that the cells were only five feet high and that offenders were passed into them sometimes through a hatchway in the pavement outside. A police station was erected in West Row in 1851 and transferred to a new building in Church Road in 1871.

The river is tidal up to Worsall – four miles above Yarm, ten above Stockton and 22 above the gares in the estuary. Before the gares there were treacherous sandbanks and these, combined with the dangers of the Tees Bay and the ubiquitous silt and sand hazards encountered en route, meant that something had to be done if river trade on the Tees was going to flourish. Two meander-eliminating cuts – Mandale and Portrack, and the estuary breakwaters – did much to improve things economically, while also shortening the distance to the sea.

For Middlesbrough, Stockton and Yarm the River Tees was central to their growth and development, and, in the case of the latter two, to their eventual decline. Stockton has been of commercial significance since the 13th century, when it filled the need for a crossing point on the trade route between Durham and York. Although it eventually developed into a bustling port, exporting wool and salmon and importing wine for the rich, Stockton for centuries was very small, with a population of around 1,000. Yarm was initially the main port where vessels of up to 65 tonnes could be accommodated, comfortably making the 23 mile voyage to the sea. In 1718 75 corn ships entered the Port of London from Stockton, more than the combined total from Sunderland and Hartlepool. By the end of the 18th century Stockton had taken over from Yarm as the principal port on the Tees; bigger boats and tides saw to that. In 1767 9,600 tons of grain, 1,400 tons of butter, cheese, pork and ham, 70 tons of ale, 900 tons of alum, and 900 tons of other products left the port. Grain was in decline, though, with 124 ships in and out in 1760, falling to 23 in 1769.

In 1810, at a dinner to celebrate the opening of a new "cut" in the River Tees, Leonard Raisbeck, the Recorder of Stockton, suggested a railway or canal to link Stockton with the "interior country". Fifteen years later, the famous Stockton & Darlington Railway opened and, on September 27th that year, a celebratory dinner took place at the town hall after George Stephenson had driven its first train into the town. The Industrial Revolution had a dramatic and pronounced effect on Stockton, changing it from a modest market town to a centre of heavy industry with the development of the railways, local ironworks and foundries, shipyards and ancillary industries dependent on these. The Portrack Iron Works opened in 1806 under Brown and Goundry; Stockton Iron Works had been opened in 1770 by John Jackson in West Row; Fossick and Hackworth started Blair's Engine Works in 1839 producing locomotives and stationary engines. Tees Glass Works opened their bottle factory in 1839. In addition, support businesses and facilities sprang up such as banks, public houses and department stores. A number of projects were completed to make Stockton more viable and attractive as a port. In 1810 The Mandale Cut was opened, constructed by the Tees Navigation Company: it cut off one of the Tees meanders, reducing the distance from the Tees Estuary to Stockton by more than two miles. Stockton's decline as a port however was caused by the opening of the railway, and by Darlington Quaker Joseph Pease, banker and coalmine owner who was also one of the promoters of and shareholders in the new railway. He was looking for a suitable site from which to export the coal, mainly to London and the south, that was cascading out of the Durham coalfields. Stockton-on-Tees had clearly now failed as a port, as bigger boats meant it was unable to cope with the increasing river trade. At the same time growing competition from the Clarence Railway on the north bank at Port Clarence was eating into its markets. In 1829 Pease sailed down the Tees, determined to find the best place for his coal staithes and with a consortium of Quaker businessmen, purchased a 527 acre farmstead and its surrounding land, described as "a dismal swamp", from William Chilton. Pease then established the Middlesbrough Estate Company or the Middlesbrough Owners. The explosive growth of Middlesbrough was assured.

Middlesbrough's population increased thirty-six fold between 1831 and 1841, from 154 to 5,463. By 1851 Middlesbrough's population was 7,600, succeeding Stockton as the principal port on the Tees. The Post Office found it hard to keep up: rivalry between the two towns was fuelled when it insisted on insulting Middlesbrough as 'Middlesbrough, near Stockton'. An adage of the time read 'Yarm was, Stockton is, Middlesbrough will be'; never were more prescient words spoken. Nevertheless, at Stockton, 150 tons and two tides was becoming the norm: Yarm declined, giving way to Stockton and later to Middlesbrough.

The Portrack Cut further reduced the distance between Stockton and Newport by three quarters of a mile and was a response to the ominous growth of Middlesbrough as a port. In the event, the increasing size of ships and the 1827 decision to extend the railway direct to Middlesbrough and so by-passing Stockton sounded the death knell for the town. The first coal staithes there were built to the west of the twenty acre site on which Middlesbrough would soon mushroom. In December 1830 the *Sunniside* sailed from Port Darlington with the first cargo of Durham coal from Middlesbrough.

A 19th century commentator floridly summed up Stockton's sad demise: 'Vessels now anchor at Middleburgh snug and comfortable, which before strove to mount the river and reach Stockton after overcoming the sad surf tossed over the bar by the easterly gales; so that Stockton as a maritime place has become insignificant'.

Although it had declined as a port, by 1867 there were three blast furnaces, 144 puddling furnaces and six finishing mills in action in Stockton. The companies were Stockton Rail Mill Co; The Malleable Iron Co; Holdsworth & Co; and the West Stockton Iron Co. They were later joined by Pickerings who manufactured lifting gear, Bowesfield Iron & Steel Co; and Lustrum Iron Works amongst others. There were more in Eaglescliffe and Thornaby. The censuses show the effect that industry had on the town's population, from 1871 in particular: population in 1801 was 4,009; in 1811, 4,229; in 1821, 5,006; in 1831 7,763; in 1841, 9,825; in 1851, 10,172; in 1861, 13,357; in 1871 it doubled to 27,738; in 1881, 41,015; in 1891, 49,659. In the years between 1801 and 1951 Stockton's population increased from 4,177 to 74,000 which is an eighteen-fold increase; Eston saw a 63 times increase while Middlesbrough showed an astonishing 6,000 times.

24 The Square in Thistle Green was home to the Quayside Mission Hall and Rescue Mission, later the Quayside Mission Men's Home – from 1903. In 1973 Remploy took over the building as a clothing factory. The Mission was founded in 1906. The census opaquely lists the residents as 'lodgers'. The Mission, formerly a manor house, charged 6d per night to 32 homeless men and doled out food to local children as well as to the men when times were worse than usual. It stood behind the cattle market and next door to a Sunday school with Housewifes Lane running off to the right behind the children. The Square also had St. Thomas C. of E. School, a pawnbroker, Kelly the Ferryman's house and the Half Moon Inn.

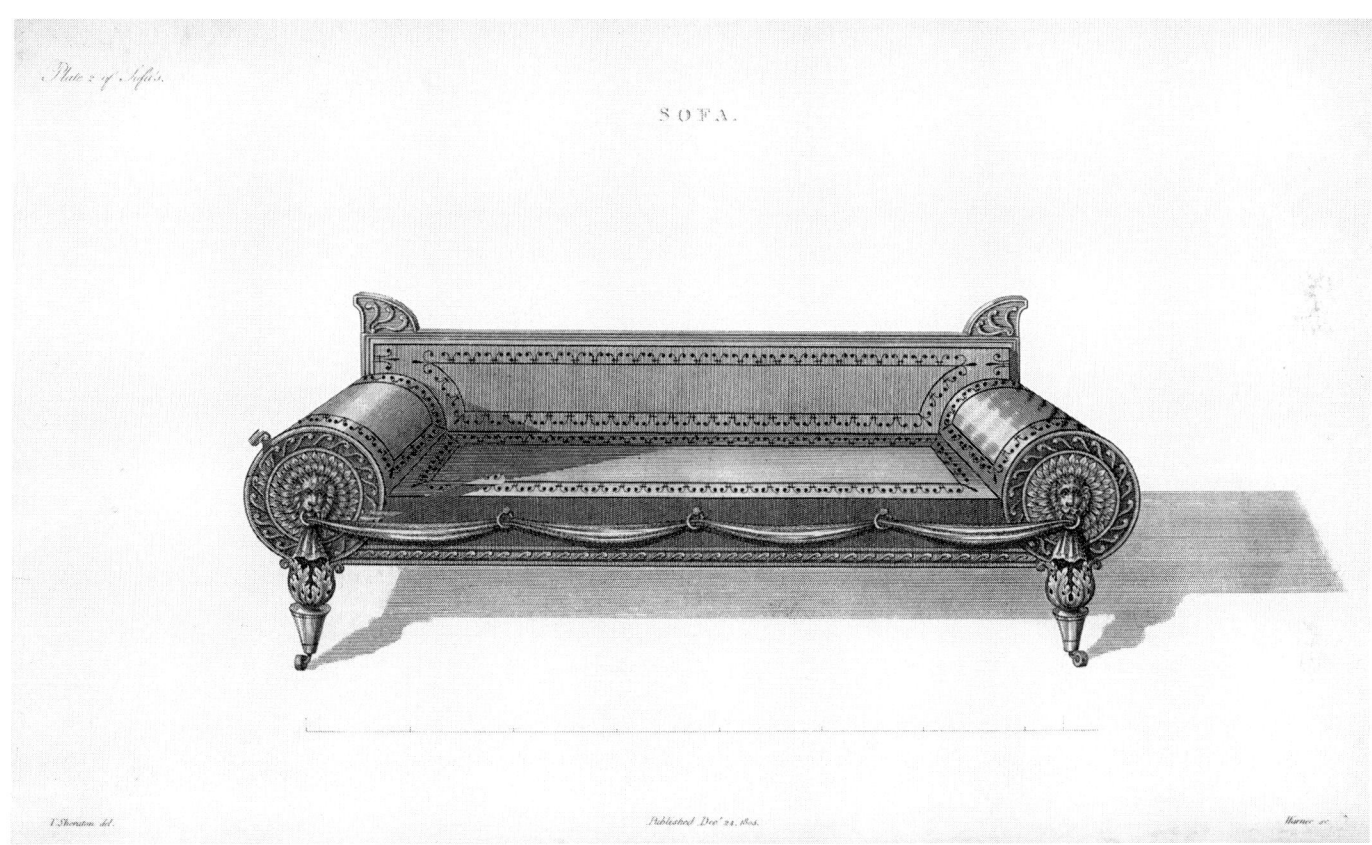

A Sheraton-style sofa, from *The Cabinet-Maker, Upholsterer and General Artist's Encyclopaedia*, 1804-07, written and designed by Thomas Sheraton. Thomas Sheraton, famous furniture maker, was born in the town in 1751 where he served his time before moving to London. He achieved no fame during his lifetime and died in poverty. A pub on Bridge Road bears his name. He authored a number of what came to be regarded as bibles for furniture designers: in 1791 the influential four volume *The Cabinet Maker's and Upholsterer's Drawing Book* was published. In 1803 he released the cutting edge *Cabinet Dictionary* a definitive rule book on the techniques of cabinet and chair making; in 1805 came the first volume of *Cabinet Maker, Upholsterer and General Artist's Encyclopaedia*. Sheraton himself never made any of the pieces described and depicted in his books and no surviving pieces of furniture can be credited to him directly. A 'Sheraton' therefore always denotes the design and not the maker. He died in Broad Street in 1806 of 'phrenitis', an inflammation of the brain accompanied by fever and delirium, leaving his wife Margaret and their two children in poverty. Sheraton was forever the bridesmaid to the likes of Otley's Chippendale, just as his hometown was to become bridesmaid to Middlesbrough.

HIGH STREET. STOCKTON-ON-TEES.

Stockton market – the life blood of the town for centuries and the largest outdoor market in the north east of England. In the early days the produce for sale came from the surrounding region: vegetables, fish, wool and the like. A light came on in Stockton in 1827 when local chemist John Walker invented the friction match in his shop at 59 High Street. He was born in Stockton in 1781 and was apprenticed to Watson Alcock, the town's principal surgeon. Walker, however, could not stomach the surgery and changed to chemistry. After studying at Durham and York, he returned to Stockton and set up as a chemist and druggist at 59 High Street around 1818.

Stockton's market on the High Street goes back to 1310 when Bishop Bek of Durham granted a market charter in perpetuity – 'to our town of Stockton a market upon every Wednesday for ever.' Collingwoods the jewellers is on the left to the right of the 'Bovril' sign; they took over the building from the E. Cowley family, who ran their watchmaker and jewellery shop on the corner of Dovecot Street – High Street (no. 131) for many years. Cowley's was on the site of Cattaneo's – jewellers and silversmiths 1879–96.

Stockton is the widest high street in the UK. The centrepiece is the Town House or town hall, which dates from 1735, and the Georgian-style Shambles Market Hall. The imposing building to the right of the parish church is the Victoria buildings, built at the beginning of the 20th century on the site of the almshouses which were relocated to the corner of Dixon and Dovecote streets.

Hiring fairs were also called statute, or mop fairs and date from the reign of Edward III (1327–77). The Statute of Apprentices of 1563 legislated for a particular day when the high constables of the shire would proclaim the stipulated rates of pay and conditions of employment for the following year. The fairs quickly turned into the place for matching workers and employers. Hiring fairs continued well into the 20th century, up to the Second World War in some places. Farm workers, labourers, servants and some craftsmen worked for their employer from October to October. At the end of their employment they would go to the mop fair in their Sunday best, carrying an item signifying their trade. A servant with no specific skills would carry a mop head: The 'tassle' everyone wore on their lapel was another emblem of the employee's trade and was known as a 'mop'. Once agreement was reached the employer would give the employee a small token of money, known as the "fasten-penny," usually a shilling, which "fastened" the contract for a year. The employee would then remove the item signifying their trade and replace it with bright ribbons to indicate they had been hired.

In the 1200s Stockton was granted borough status with the Crown allowing it self-governance. The borough was controlled by the Bishop of Durham who developed the wide High Street lined with tenements or burgages on either side. The burgages comprised a commercial property fronting directly on to the High Street while at the rear would be yards and outbuildings for commercial and industrial activity. This pattern of long narrow plots with rear yards is still in evidence in the town today. Burgage holders would pay rent to the Bishop and were taxed on the goods bought and sold. In a survey of 1382 there were 46 recorded burgage tenements. Yards included Wasp Nest Yard, Hambletonian Yard, Ship Inn Yard and Green Dragon Yard which is home to the Green Dragon pub, the Green Dragon Studios (recording studios) and the Georgian Theatre. The Town House is visible at the end of the street.

The Empire was the Castle Theatre from 1907 to 1912. It was demolished in the 1970s and replaced by the Swallow Hotel. The Georgian Theatre at Green Dragon Yard is also Grade II listed and is the oldest Georgian theatre in the country. Opened in 1766, it fell into disrepair during the 19th century and later was used as a sweet factory and then a community building. The Globe Theatre, also in the High Street, is Grade II listed and was built in 1936 on the same site as two previous theatres. It has hosted many famous acts such as Buddy Holly, the Rolling Stones, the Animals, Cilla Black, Carl Perkins and Chuck Berry. The Beatles famously played the Globe on Friday 22nd November 1963, the day Kennedy was assassinated. Binns is advertised on the tram, the department store of choice here and in Sunderland, Darlington, West Hartlepool and Middlesbrough where there were branches.

Shipbuilding began in the mid 17th century with 60 ships built between 1780 and 1800; the yards were at Smithfield and near to Stockton Bridge. The first iron ship turned out here was a screw steamer, *The Advance*, built at South Stockton in 1854 by the Iron Shipbuilding Company, later the aptly-named Richardson, Duck and Co; by 1865 they had launched 80 vessels, 50 of which were steamers. At the same time, Pearse, Lockwood & Co in Ropner's Yard launched 64 including 34 steamers. The first steel ship was *Little Lucy* built in 1858. Pearse launched their largest steamer, the 377 feet *Talpore* in 1860 – a troop ship which was dismantled, shipped and reassembled in India where it saw action on the River Indus; it was the world's largest river steamer at the time. Ships' boilers were much in demand, leading local firm Fossick's to move into marine engineering from 1853.

Steam trams began running in the streets in 1881 and were replaced by electric trams in 1897. Buses replaced the trams in 1931. The Middlesbrough, Stockton & Thornaby Electric Tramways Company operated an electric tramway service between Middlesbrough, Thornaby-on-Tees, Stockton-on-Tees and Norton between 1898 and 1921. Before 1898 the Imperial Tramways Company had been snapping up local tramway companies in the area, and once these were all under its control, it combined these as a unified system to connect Middlesbrough and Stockton. From Norton Green, the former steam tram route was extended beyond Thornaby to Newport, and the former horse tram route was made to reach beyond Middlesbrough Town Hall to Borough Road East. From Middlesbrough Railway Station the line extended beyond Benson Street, to Roman Road. Services started on 16th July 1898. One further extension from Middlesbrough Railway Station to the ferry opened on 16th August 1901. The depot was located off Boathouse Lane.

Stockton Parish Church (in the distance) was completely rebuilt in the 1730s. The muddy streets had been paved in 1717. The photo dates from about 1895.

Locomotion No. 1 of the Stockton & Darlington Railway at their 1925 100th anniversary cavalcade. The 100 year old locomotive is indeed hauling the train, although it was propelled by a small petrol engine in its replica tender while the chimney smoke was created from burning oily rags. Once the railway had opened, the price of coal at Stockton dropped from 18s to 8s 6d per ton and allowed coal to be shipped expediently from the pits of south-west Durham to Pease's staithes at Stockton: coal was being exported from Stockton within four months. Before the railway received its locomotives to run on the line, contractors fixed flanges to the wheels of their carts and coaches and used it as a road. The first ship to leave the Tees with a cargo of coal was the *Adamant* towed by the steam tug *Albion*. Two years later there were five staithes on the Tees below the site of what had once been Stockton Castle.

The Hetton Loco in 1925 at the centenary celebrations for the opening of the Stockton and Darlington Railway. The Inspector for the railway, Robert Henry Layton is on the footplate with the driver and fireman.

The railway station in the 1920s. Seventy years earlier the Leeds Northern Railway (LNR), originally the Leeds and Thirsk Railway from 1849, extended its route northwards from Melmerby to Billingham-on-Tees via Northallerton and Eaglescliffe. Stockton-on-Tees was one of the intermediate stations on the route opening on 2nd June 1852; that same year it was renamed North Stockton. On 1st November 1892 it was given its original name which remained until 1985 when British Rail abbreviated it to Stockton. To the dismay of many the current station as pictured is not at the same place as the famous former terminus of the Stockton and Darlington Railway although they share the same name; this was constructed in 1892/93 by the NER to replace the earlier one referred to above, which was shared by the LNR and the Stockton and Hartlepool Railway.

As with towns up and down the country, women suddenly became 'temporary men' in 1914 when they were called on to stand in for the predominantly male industrial workforce. They drove and conducted trams and worked in factories, often as munitionettes in arms and weapon-filling factories. This was dangerous and demanding work with the added vulnerability to industrial diseases caused by the toxic explosives they worked with. These women war workers are in Thornaby engine sheds. After the war they would, like most women war workers, have been laid off and returned to their kitchens to give way to the returning troops.

Huge increases in Stockton's population in the 19th century were accompanied by high levels of poverty and insanitary living. This shows life in Constable's Yard in the hideous Thistle Green area of the town which at one time had been fashionable. Mason's Yard and Housewife's Lane were two other wretched slums, the former running from the Shambles in the High Street to the river, the latter past the Baltic Tavern towards the river at Hubback's Quay. The terrible 1832 cholera outbreak killed 126 people; a further twenty died seventeen years later in the 1849 outbreak. Gas lit the town from 1822 but a hospital was not built until 1862.

Shipbuilding had initially been Stockton's forte; it started in the 15th century and reached a peak in the 17th and 18th centuries. In 1470 a wooden ship was commissioned for the Bishop of Durham, using 32 stones of iron fashioned into nails at six and half pennies per stone. Between 1790 and 1805 Thomas Haw was building ships which saw action in the Napoleonic wars. Three shipping companies were formed between 1822 and 1835: by then 272 ships with a combined tonnage of 51,000 were registered at Stockton, exporting coal mainly; none survived the impending surging rise of Middlesbrough. This photo from about 1875 is at Corporation Quay. On 1st January 1967 Stockton Corporation Quay passed over to the newly-formed Tees and Hartlepools Port Authority who closed the wharf to commercial traffic that September.

Shipbuilding acted as a magnet for smaller industries such as brick, sailcloth and rope making which is remembered today in local names such as Ropery Street. Just how important rope making was to the town is underlined by the fact that in 1825 1,178 tons of hemp were landed at Stockton. Cotton was important too: a cotton mill was established in 1839 and the Stockton Sugar Refinery had set up at 'Sugar House Open' – the only sugar refinery between Hull and Newcastle. There was thriving brick-making in Stockton too – bricks were much in demand as towns continued to spring up in the region and with them the urgent need for houses and other buildings. The clay used for the bricks also found a market in the hugely important local pottery industry: 1825 saw William Smith open his Stafford Pottery at South Stockton (Thornaby), a new town; in 1860 his brother James opened a pottery factory called the North Shore Pottery. Others included the Ainsworth's white and printed ware pottery of North Stockton and the Harwoods Norton Pottery specialising in `Sunderland Ware'. Other 'Owners of the Thornaby Estate' (Smith's consortium) enterprises included the short-lived Thornaby Cotton Mill and the successful Thornaby Iron Works. Stockton then was the principal port for County Durham, Yorkshire's North Riding and even Westmorland, mainly exporting rope, agricultural produce and lead from the Yorkshire Dales, trading extensively with the Baltic states.

The *Stella Mary* was owned by J. G. Peckston Ltd, Transport House, Middlesbrough from 1954 to 1961 when she was sold to Chr. M. Sarlis & Co, Piraeus and renamed *Ilona* registered at Patras. There was also a *Judith Mary*; among other destinations they sailed from Stockton to Finland and occasionally to Ireland.

The stone five arch Stockton Bridge was completed in 1771 and was toll free by 1820. Before this bridge cross-river traffic was provided for by Bishop's Ferry. Stockton Bridge replaced Yarm Bridge in Yarm as the lowest bridging point on the River Tees.

The low-level Victoria Bridge was built by way of an 1881 Act of Parliament and was constructed (1882–87) at a cost of £69,051, financed by the local council, a tramway company, the North Eastern Railway and the water board and commemorates the 50th year of the reign of Queen Victoria. The tram system was soon extended over the bridge and was the lowest permanent bridge point until the opening of the Tees Newport Bridge in 1934. During the Second World War a bomb smashed through the roadway without exploding – the evidence can still be seen in bomb case shrapnel on the bridge.

The large building giving off smoke is the North of England Pure Oil Cake Company (1869) which processed linseed and cotton seed. To the right is the Bridge Hotel in Thornaby, demolished in 1970.

The discovery of the match was all rather serendipitous: John Walker had been routinely selling concoctions of combustible materials in powder form to smokers and to a gunsmith; in 1826 he was experimenting with these combustibles when, by chance, he scraped the mixing stick against his hearth and the stick caught fire. Samples were distributed locally while Walker perfected his invention: sulphur, tipped with a mixture of sulphide of antimony, chlorate of potash, and gum, on the end of a stick, were sold as friction matches and supplied with a piece of folded sandpaper as the scraping agent. He called the matches 'Congreves' in homage to the rocket pioneer, Sir William Congreve. Walker's daybook initially described the phenomenon as 'Sulphurata Hyper-Oxygenata Fric' which, no doubt for sound branding reasons, he renamed as the more pithy `Friction Lights'. His first matches were made of pasteboard, later replaced with three inch wood splints cut by elderly people hired by the chemist. In 1830 enter an intrigued Michael Faraday who came to visit urging Walker to apply for a patent. The reasonably well off Walker did nothing and inevitably a man called Samuel Johnson took out a patent for 'Friction Matches', branding the matches as 'Lucifers'. The devil, as ever, is in the detail…. Walker died in 1859 aged 78 sans brevet and is buried in St. Mary's Church in Norton.

In 1871 council minutes noted 'it was ordered that a Committee be appointed to consider the question of providing a proper Fire Brigade for the town'. A horse-drawn steam powered fire engine, built by Merryweather and Sons, was duly purchased and helmets of 'leather, brass-mounted', were provided for the firemen. Corporation premises in West Row, then occupied by the Stockton Rifle Volunteer Corps, were converted to an engine house together with stables and a coach-house nearby. In May 1872 six men were appointed as paid firemen – an engine man, a stoker, a driver, one leading fireman and two firemen, each paid a retainer to be available for 'call-outs'. In 1879, the building in West Row was connected with the South Stockton Police Station, and with the private fire brigade at Blair's Works 'by telegraph wire'. In May 1873, call boys were being used to call out members of the Brigade and by the end of 1875 a new manual fire engine and a fire escape were bought. By 1877 the bell in the town hall clock tower was being used to call out the Brigade, but not for long as ringing the bell not only summoned them, but also anyone else who felt like some free entertainment, impeding the firemen as they rushed to the fires. This is the horse-drawn engine of 1906.

Stockton Bowling Club started in 1895 on a flat green in Norton before later moving to Norton Road in Stockton. This photo dates from 1908. Who knows what the photographer said to them; it certainly wasn't 'Smile'. The rival Stockton West End Bowling Club was founded in 1903 but it really started at Ropner Park when it opened its first bowling green in 1893. By early 1895 Ropner Park Bowling Club was established. In 1903 it was the West End Bowling Club, now in Darlington Road.

What looks like the whole of Stockton singing the National Anthem at the 1911 Coronation of King George V and Queen Mary. Hepworth's is on the left. Stockton Literary and Philosophical Institute, on the right, was built in 1839 as a Corporation Hall and became the Literary and Philosophical Institute in 1851 in a bid to establish a library and a museum for the town. In 1883 it was rebadged as the Stockton Institute of Literature and Science. By 1889 it was known as the Stockton Literary Institute. It was the *Northern Echo* office from 1900 until 1964 when it was demolished.

This photo of Langholm Walk could have been taken in any number of council estates, certainly in the north east; I lived in one just like this in Hartlepool. The younger children sidelined on the right won't be going in to bat or bowl. Did the girl at the back get a game? In December 2018 a three bedroomed terrace in Langholm Walk sold for £110,000. By the late 1970s almost a third of UK households lived in social housing. From the 1950s for many 'working-class' people, this housing model provided their first experience of private indoor toilets, bathrooms and hot running water, as well as gardens and electric lighting. For tenants in England and Wales it also usually provided the first experience of private garden space (usually front and rear).

A welcome awaits you at Jas. Smith hardware shop in November 1966.

J Smith in Georgina Street, Thornaby about 1904. In the mid '40s this was a sweet shop.

The horse-drawn contraption is possibly a reaper-binder. The binder was invented in 1872 by Charles Baxter Withington, a jeweller from Janesville, Wisconsin. As well as cutting the small-grain crop, the binder also 'binds' the stems into bundles or sheaves. These sheaves are usually then 'shocked' into A-shaped conical stooks, resembling small tepees, to allow the grain to dry for several days before being picked up and threshed. The tarpaulin was made by Blakeborough & Rhodes of 57 High Street Stockton, who were hot water engineers and also specialised in hearths, fenders, wrought iron fencing and gates. More interesting were their coal vases, kitchen ranges, tiled register stoves, artistic mantelpieces in wood, iron, slate and marble.

Wharton Bros. King Street – hairdressers catering for ladies and gents. The two smart men may well be the brothers Wharton themselves. The salon was opposite the famous Stockton Modeller in Silver Street – beloved of every Stockton-Norton boy and girl. Above the barber's was Hartlepool Mutual Trading Company: here the reps used to offer coupons to people who did not always not have the cash to buy clothing, for example. The clients paid the coupon back at so much a week. Note the advert for 'Marcel Waving', Evan Williams original shampoos and the offer to extract your corns…

A somewhat unhappy looking lady, to say the least, at the wheel of a seven hp Little Star at Low Row. The car was registered in Newcastle to Alfred John Nathan Smithson of Stockton – an inveterate car collector who had owned over 100 vehicles by 1968.

Norton is of Anglo-Saxon origin, developing into a market town. For centuries the parish included Stockton, but this status was reversed in 1913 when Norton became part of the borough of Stockton-on-Tees. Despite its leafy character, Norton had its fair share of industry: there was a brick works, the Clarence Pottery and the Clarence Windmill. Westminster's Big Ben's first bell was cast by John Warner & Sons in Norton in 1856; it was tested and found to be perfect but there was a delay of sixteen months in having it fitted and it was then found to be fractured. A farm called Holm House was near the old Portrack meander of the River Tees; in the 18th century it was the home of Thomas Baker, farmer Quaker and preacher who became known as 'Potato Tom' for introducing the potato to County Durham at Norton in about 1736 – Norton's own Sir Walter Raleigh. Holm House is long gone but its site in part is occupied by the Holme House Prison built in 1992. In 1982 human bones were discovered by schoolchildren near the Mill Lane area of the village; an Anglo-Saxon pagan cemetery was subsequently unearthed. Excavations in 1984 revealed 120 burials (117 inhumations and three cremations) in graves that contained personal items such as spears, belt buckles, tweezers and brooches dating to around AD 540–610. The photo shows The Green about 1900 with West Row, Ragworth Hall, and, in the distance, Darlington Lane.

The fourteen cottage style Fox almshouses off the High Street were founded in 1897 at the bequest of local brewer John Henry Fox whose will directed that the business be discontinued and the brewery razed to the ground. Nine pubs were sold by the trustees in 1894. Certainly closing time here then.

J.M. Gaskill's grocer shop with an impressive clock around 1900 with the Hambletonian Inn just visible on the left. In 1891 the *London Gazette* published a receiving order against Robert Procter, innkeeper, who had since moved to Greatham near West Hartlepool. The Hambletonian Inn was on the same block as the blacksmiths opposite Norton duck pond. The inn closed and it became Miss Foster's paper and sweet shop before the war. The Unicorn is where it always was on the corner before the Green. It was also known as Dobbies after landlord Albert Dobson. After he died his wife took over and then it was Nellies – life was so simple then. Red House School, an independent school, was established here in 1929 by a group of parents.

The tram nearest to the camera in Norton High Street is advertising Vaux's Stout – Vaux were a Sunderland brewery. Originally steam-driven trams owned by the Middlesbrough and Stockton Tram Company ran from Norton village green at the Hambletonian Inn to Thornaby; they were taken over in 1896 by the Imperial Tramway Company who electrified the system and joined it with Middlesbrough and North Ormesby. The trams ran up the change line from Stockton, the driver moved the pick-up arm from one end to the other and then, after changing the points, ran back towards Stockton. Trams ran from Norton until the end of 1931.

Thornaby was born about AD 800 when the land on which it stands was given by Halfdan Ragnarsson, King of the Danes, to Thormod, one of his noblemen, giving us "Thormods-by" – Thormod's farm. However, life here goes back a lot further when prehistoric man eked out a living: a stone axe, eight inches long has been found, dating back to the Mesolithic Period (about 10,000 BC to 8,000 BC). In 1926, a dugout canoe said to date from between 1600–1400 BC was found in the mud under eight feet of water opposite Thornaby High Wood. An arrowhead of the Neolithic Period (around 10,000 BC until 3,000 BC) was found in a garden on Thornaby Village Green. The name Thornaby has had a number of variants over the centuries including Turmozbi, Tormozbi, Tormozbia and Thurmozbi. By the 1820s Thornaby, centred around St. Peter's Church and the ancient village green, was overshadowed by the newly-named town of South Stockton two miles away on the Yorkshire side of the River Tees opposite Stockton-on-Tees. It was originally named Mandale – a separate settlement from Thornaby. In 1825 South Stockton saw the establishment of William Smith's pottery with shipbuilding and engineering following. On 6th October 1892 South Stockton and Old Thornaby merged to form the municipal borough of Thornaby-on-Tees. Victoria Bridge opened on 20th June 1887 to commemorate the Golden Jubilee of Queen Victoria and replaced an earlier bridge of 1771.

Five Lamps, Thornaby-on-Tees.

The Five Lamps with Thornaby Town Hall in the background and the Conservative Club on the right. Robert de Thormodbi (Thornaby) was wounded in the Crusades at Acre in the 13th century; he swore to raise a shrine to the Virgin Mary if he survived his wounds. Survive he did, and as part of his oath a shrine niche to the Virgin Mary, lit by five sanctuary lamps, was placed in St. Peter's Church. The lamps now on Mitchell Avenue, next to Acklam Road were first erected in 1874 at the junction of Mandale Road and George Street. A replica set was made by the apprentices at Head Wrightson engineering company and sited in Westbury Street to make way for the A66.

Thornaby Station lies on the original Stockton & Darlington Railway (S&DR) extension to Port Darlington, developed from 1828 by Joseph Pease. March 1907 saw a mineral train travelling from Stockton and comprising 30-ton wagons and a goods train collide here when one of the wagons jumped the tracks only to hit the goods train coming in the opposite direction and travelling about 15 miles per hour. No one was seriously injured in the crash but several people suffered bruises and shock.

Thomas Whitewell was the younger brother of William Whitwell – in 1859 they were co-founders of the Thornaby Ironworks shown here. After a serious fire in South Stockton in 1876, Thomas Whitwell suggested that they should have their own fire brigade and he was tasked with its formation. On August 5th 1878, Thomas was called to the works to inspect a faulty furnace. He and his foreman, John Thompson, climbed down into the ashpit of the furnace only to be met by a blast of escaping steam which badly scalded them both. They managed to climb from the furnace but both died of their burns later that day. Stockton Fire Brigade had lost its first captain, not on duty at a blaze but at his own ironworks.

Head Wrightson was a major employer in Thornaby. In the 1950s, the boilers for the Bradwell nuclear power plant were too big to transport by road from Thornaby, so Head Wrightson launched them into the Tees then onto Teesport. The firm specialised in the manufacture of very large industrial products made of cast iron or wrought iron; they were used for boilers, railway engines, navy ships, and many bridges around the world. Their story starts in 1840 when as Head Ashby, on land in Thornaby Carrs, they manufactured cotton for ships' sails. In 1859 Thomas Head and Joseph Wright took over the Teesdale Iron Works founded in 1840 and which built Teeside's first blast furnace in 1851. When Wright retired, confusingly, Thomas Wrightson joined the firm which in 1865 thus became Messrs. Head Wrightson & Co. Ltd employing 450 people. In 1866 the name shortened to Head Wrightson. In 1877 they completed the Chenab Bridge in India and in 1889 Fulham Railway Bridge. By 1892 the firm employed 1,200 people.

In 1896 the company acquired Stockton Forge Works in Norton Road, shown here in the 1920s, enabling the company to expand rapidly. By the early 20th century practically every blast furnace on the North East coast (and there were many, from Redcar to Newcastle) was built by Head Wrightson. The company took over the Stockton Steel Foundry plant to extend steel castings in 1929. During the 1920s and 1930s the company expanded still further until by the 1940s the Head Wrightson Works at Thornaby, Middlesbrough and Seaton Carew covered a total of 70 acres and employed over 4,500 people. But it was not always boom time in Stockton: in 1931, during the previous great economic slump, the Wrightson family had to mortgage their mansion, Neasham Hall near Darlington, to save the firm from going under. In the Second World War they manufactured the Bellman hangar at RAF Thornaby, a 1936 design for a standard transportable aeroplane shed for the Air Ministry. 1965 saw their building of the Billingham Forum ice rink. In 1968 the firm employed nearly 6,000 people over six Teesside sites and mostly made boilers and other heavy engineering. Davy Corporation acquired Head Wrightson in 1977 and closed it in June 1987.

Working on Impeller Moulds in the foundry, July 1962, while wearing shirt, tie and waistcoat. *Head Wrightson Photographic Archive*.

106 Squadron Handley Page Hampden L4178, RAF Thornaby-on-Tees, Yorkshire 1939. The Squadron converted from Fairey Battles to the HP Hampden in 1939; by May it had sixteen Hampdens. RAF Thornaby closed in October 1958 when the Hawker Hunters of 92 Squadron decamped to RAF Middleton St. George.

Thornaby was a significant air base; the Royal Flying Corps, Fighter Command, Bomber Command and Coastal Command all operated from Thornaby over the years, but its work under Coastal Command is what the base was famous for, particularly in its air-sea rescue role and the development of the Thornaby Bag – an emergency bag dropped to aircrew downed at sea which contained food, cigarettes and drink. The aerodrome opened on 29th September 1929, although aviation in Thornaby dates back to 1912 when Gustav Hamel used Vale Farm for a flying display. Subsequently the Royal Flying Corps used the same fields as a staging post between Catterick and Marske Aerodromes between 1914 and 1918. Thornaby became a fully operational RAF station when a station headquarters was established on 1st June 1937.

The Airmen memorial at Thornaby on the site of the former RAF Thornaby, erected 1997; in 2007 a full-size replica Spitfire aircraft was erected on the roundabout at the junction of Thornaby Road, Bader Avenue and Trenchard Avenue.

The day the piano had to go – at the Alma Hotel. Nancy Skelton (née Brigham) was part of the Audrey Bailey Dance School; she later had a successful career as a singer and toured with the Kay Sisters for a while. Her father Eric Brigham, whose name is over the door, ran the Alma Hotel and later the Bridge Hotel in Thornaby. Maybe that piano was Nancy's.

Up on the roof above the High Street.

Stockton Racecourse was never in Stockton. It was actually in Thornaby, but was once considered 'the finest in the north'. At one point racing became so popular that every August, local factories closed down for Stockton Race Week. Its demise began after the Second World War; the last race was run in June 1981. Racing took place at three sites in Thornaby: Mandale Carrs, from 1724 until 1816; from September 1855 at Mandale Marshes, situated in a loop in the River Tees – in three days racing in 1864 the attendance was 36,000. Racing at Stockton was exclusively on the flat until the opening of the national hunt course in 1967.